TAILS

To Fiona and Peter,

With much love

from

Kona

KONA MACPHEE

Tails

BLOODAXE BOOKS

ISBN: 1 85224 660 X

First published 2004 by
Bloodaxe Books Ltd,
Highgreen,
Tarset,
Northumberland NE48 1RP.

www.bloodaxebooks.com
For further information about Bloodaxe titles
please visit our website or write to
the above address for a catalogue.

Bloodaxe Books Ltd acknowledges
the financial assistance of
Arts Council England, North East.

Cover printing by J. Thomson Colour Printers Ltd, Glasgow.

Printed in Great Britain by
Cromwell Press Ltd, Trowbridge, Wiltshire.

For k

Acknowledgements

Acknowledgements are due to the editors of the following publications in which some of these poems first appeared: *Acumen*, *Anvil New Poets*, edited by Roddy Lumsden and Hamish Ironside (Anvil Press Poetry, 2001), *Poetry Wales*, *Reactions* (Pen&inc, 2000), *Staying Alive: real poems for unreal times*, edited by Neil Astley (Bloodaxe Books, 2002) and *The Wolf*. 'Flying' was commissioned by Shakespeare's Globe for *'Earth has not any thing to shew more fair'*, edited by Peter Oswald, Alice Oswald and Robert Woof (Shakespeare's Globe & the Wordsworth Trust, 2002).

Thanks are due to the Society of Authors for an Eric Gregory Award in 1998.

Contents

TAILS

god how he sings

the robin(who
'll be silent in
a moon or two)

E.E. CUMMINGS

Taking her in
(for Fiona)

You're taking her in, your mottled little sister,
splayed on the lap of the capable nurse
with relatives flanking her fever. Outside
late November is leaf-fall and frost,
the ground blotchy, matching her face
for raddled texture, the close of a season.

Tilted aslant to the window, you're playing
a game with your eyes, you're trying to catch
the car becalmed, the world in progress
backwards, the other way, back home.
You're not there yet, not nearly there
when the nurse looks up. *She's gone. I'm so sorry.*

The car stops. Your breath stops. Everything stops.
Such stillness in that car, you'd swear it's there
for good, you feel the stalled wheels sinking anchors.
Your uncle gets out, seeking a telephone,
seeking advice, and you see the adults
are no more certain than you what comes now.

Uphill, a postman cycles past – the one
who gave her peppermints, who'll take a cord
and guide her through that fine slot into earth?
He glides on the skyline, his cobweb wheels
tumbling against his progress, and is gone.
You stare as though he might spool by again.

It's colder, darker, and now there's a wind.
You're glad of the hood of the car, a shield
to the cryptically gesturing skeleton trees.
You wish you could drag that steel lid lower,
wear it like a carapace, a metal skin,
haul your limbs and head and heart right in.

Finally, your uncle returns: the door
squeals on its ailing hinge. There's a pause;
nobody speaks; you hear his loops of breath
as you, he, all of you, reel yourselves in.
At last he turns to the seats behind.
We'll go back, he says. But of course you can't.

My people

my people
pass through gardens untouched by the toxic pollen of lilies
sway with the pre-factored rhythm of skyscrapers flexing in strong wind
thicken the air at night clubs and bus stops and cab ranks with their
    absence

my people
speak with the voices of ten million leaves, of earthquakes and dust motes
feed on starlight and moonshine and fallen crumbs of consumed dreams
grow with the vegetable fierceness of beansprouts, knowing that no
    growing is death

when they come
outracing planes whose snail trails silver the hollow sphere of the air
from earth where coal can burn twenty years in an underground seam
by sea, with sodium fire in their radiant lungfuls of water

their hands
will greet me with gestures that flux into silent legions of butterflies
will bear astounding weight with the sevenfold strength of ants
will move over me like perfect maggots purging the flesh of wounds

my people
are moving somewhere, trailing in wakes of their purpose the seasons
are wrung by an appetite gnawing at glaciers and atoms and bricks
are tirelessly looking for me, but in the wrong house, or country, or
    century

Terminus

A raven's restless mechanism
ticks on the signal box. Below,
midday sinuates the sheets of air
that work their quavering mesmerism,
dazing the land to stillness. Here
beside the fenceline's silted flow,

wheatstalks perpendict the lines
whose rusting railtops flash quick bronze
with flicking skinks, the sleepers, stones,
slowly weathering beneath them. Signs
have lost their lettering, blank as bones.
A peppercorn tree, some kurrajongs,

slip their roots beneath the rails
and scatter leaves and shadows. Boles
that brace the sky-flecked roof are scored
with tracks of borers, spiralled trails
that dwindle, disappear, record
a distant passage. Quick patrols

of ants dissect a fallen moth,
freighting it piecewise down the run
of pheromones that won't outlast
their usefulness. Green overgrowth
lies heavily, like something cast
to drip and dry in midday sun.

Perspective's engine hauls the eyes
along the single-gauge, the groove
of jumbling rocks, which slant toward
a station hidden past the sliced
horizon. Here, no train to board.
The hot air shimmers. Nothing moves.

IVF

I come home early, feel the pale house close
around me as the pressure of my blood
knocks at my temples, feel it clench me in
its cramping grasp, the fierceness of its quiet
sanctioning the small and listless hope
that I might find it mercifully empty.

Dazed, I turn the taps to fill the empty
tub, and draw the bathroom door to close
behind me. I lie unmoving, feel all hope
leaching from between my legs as blood
tinges the water, staining it the quiet
shade of a winter evening drifting in

on sunset. Again, no shoot of life sprouts in
this crumbling womb that wrings itself to empty
out the painfully-planted seeds. The quiet
doctors, tomorrow, will check their notes and close
the file, wait for the hormones in my blood
to augur further chances, more false hope.

My husband holds to patience, I to hope,
and yet our clockworks are unwinding. In
the stillness of the house, we hear our blood
pumped by hearts that gall themselves, grow empty:
once, this silence, shared, could draw us close
that now forebodes us with a desperate quiet.

I hear him at the door, but I lay quiet,
as if, by saying nothing, I may hope
that somehow his unknowingness may close
a door on all the darkness we've let in:
the nursery that's seven years too empty;
the old, unyielding stains of menstrual blood.

Perhaps I wish the petitioning of my blood
for motherhood might falter and fall quiet,
perhaps I wish that we might choose to empty
our lives of disappointment, and of hope,
but wishes founder – we go on living in
the shadow of the cliffs now looming close:

the blood that's thick with traitorous clots of hope;
the quiet knack we've lost, of giving in;
the empty room whose door we cannot close.

The fosterling

Frightened of the dark, he likes my greenhouse
for its window-walls, all bright all day.
He hides there in a stripling forest
of orchid-blades: the sprays of flowers stoop
on long stems to kiss his sandy hair.

We've learned to choose to leave him there
as long as he wants to stay, with damp air,
bagged earth, with whole and broken pots,
with all the thousand things he doesn't say.

Spring window

Raindrops finger
slight new leaves:
ghostly player-
piano keys.

Summer broods
in embryo plum
pinking on
the new-sprung stem.

Paul's epiphany

Here in the marshes, next to where
the town is moored, a noose of light
ensnares her ring

and Paul, the sharp-eyed, motors off
across the knee-deep shallows, stalls
above her, shocked to find awry
the fragile calibrations of
a living thing;

he rolls her, gently, with a foot
as if she dreams amid the mire
and might be woken, raises silt
that veils her skin

in cloudiness, her face a hint
of bones in checkmate, broken rules
beyond his ken –

and as he dangles, dumbly, there
the skin of water over her
suddenly is fleshed with pores:
a mist of rain

is falling, blurs her colours blue
and grey. Paul stands, and barely breathes,
and feels his childhood hazing out
as if a stain

is spreading, now, to saturate
the porous paper of his heart
through every vein,

and wonders if each fragile stitch
that seams the drizzled sky to ground
will hold the strain.

Flying to London

In the air two hours, at my left hand
I watched the sunset's awning-blinds unroll
across the Great Red Centre's rusty folds,
tracing a bas-relief of sky and ground.
Between those lines that marked us outward-bound,
I read a truth my country won't be told:
what foreignness our textbook England holds
couldn't be less like home than this harsh land.
In fogless dawn, real London scrolls below
and wrests itself from History and Lit
with houses ranked grey row, grey row, grey row
and proto-traffic stacking on the streets.
The seatbelt light comes on; the plane banks low;
its engines spill a last Australian heat.

Hugh's boomerang

A haze of eucalyptus oil
in sun-fermented vapour dazes
khaki trees to blue

and lubricates the air; a hunting
boomerang slips through it, winging
skew as a drunken fruitbat,

its barely slowing *whuh whuh whuh*
two coarse-thewed copter blades come loose.
A hunter's lethal spiral

is spun here to a tourist's toy
skimming the foreign green of trees
that know a leaner sun.

(O land of subtle colours, land
of larger air, you cannot catch:
I was not cleanly thrown.)

Elegy for a climber

(i.m. Brendan Murphy)

The news came plunging through the telephone
of the avalanche. He was cleaved to its heart,
his body not recovered: that death, alone,
was no more imaginable than my own.

Tirelessly, these nights, he scales again
the escarpments of my dreams: the snow-dense cloud
wakes me, shaking, defenceless, when
it cataracts down toward the small, dark men.

Summer must follow the winter freeze,
hard ice thaw, and the seasonal rivers
flood with snowmelt, bearing to the seas
a deliquescent landscape's slopes and crevices;

from his cool storage, then, he will come
to me, come home to me, at last be freed
from the airless pressure of snowflake tons,
his summits overtopped, his ascents undone.

Year Nine

(for J.R.)

Eight years the particles of virus drifted
within the bounds of his blinded eye.
We waited, hoped; the doctors' crystal
balls were masked in a wash of white.
Year Nine brought snow, and the winter light
leavened the loosened sky that piled
on rooves and branches. We exhaled
condensing residues of breath that veiled
our visions, and our presciences failed –

yet who could guess that a ball of snow
so innocently thrown, might glance against
his healthy eye, and wake the virus there?
The following day, that stricken eye rose
to an ominous dawn, a spreading flush of red
that stained the white, foretold the rise
of viral ascendancy in sky-blue eyes.

Steadily, that ice-sharp year, the virus
tightened its milky blinkers round
his sight. The dimness gradually condensed
until, on the dregs of a pallid autumn,
the winter settled in, solidified the dark.
The doctors put aside their needles and their doubts;
our tunnel-vision's last light coldly faded out.
By then we were frozen, and our icicle hearts
shattered in that winter's terminating blow:
his memory of white in the cold sting of snow.

Hortus Botanicus

The bees in bands of honey-brown and black
thrum from wood-walled boxes, rumble back

like a pollen train, haul after yellow haul,
to the work concealed behind the beehive walls.

The Hortus rings the beehives like a garland
and no bee ventures further, to the Holland

Theatre, shrugs its polychrome array
to strip grey pollen from the grey bouquet

that's held by the girl in the wedding dress,
a grey star stitched to her white left breast.

What need have bees to plague the pale bride
who bears her own plague-mark, there on her left side,

when downstairs, out, and back along the road,
the daffodils bow beneath their shocking gold?

The Amsterdam Hortus Botanicus is found on Plantage Middenlaan,
just down from the Holland Theatre, deportation point for Amsterdam
Jews in 1942-44 and now a Jewish war memorial and historical museum.

The pit

Centuries ago, there'd been a pit
where townsfolk cast the carcasses of beasts:
the long haul, the heave or roll,
the quick dispatch of lime, the quick retreat.
Nearing that pit, a skittish horse
would baulk and flicker eye-whites at the stench.

The pit-man worked with pole and spade
to clear fresh space, level the stiffened limbs.
Some rare mornings as he plied his pole
he'd turn a flank of dog or sheep
and find an infant squirreled underneath.
These he took up gently with the spade
and buried in the night behind his mangels.

The sanitary Victorians filled it in
with light earth and more bone-scouring lime,
slabbed right over its secrets and its stink
with three flat storeys of a house:
but secrets always out. The white walls
skew and crack now on the shifting ground;
the doors stick in their crooked frames;
the windows jam. The listing of the house
impels us downward, down to beast and bone.

it's 4:17 AM

and he's on his left side   dreaming of docks
where mist curls like a bad thriller
    where he's mr macho   mr trilby-and-trenchcoat
    waiting with fat insouciant cigar
to bag a load of illicit cargo

    when a torch winks twice   an arranged sign
to prowl the stacked container rows
for the one that's waiting   marked XXX
    or sealed with painted kisses   and he snicks
the old lock with his cigar cutter
    breaks it off   hauls back the door

    and a shoal of Bangkok Ladyboys tips out
like festoon streamers from a sprung tin
    all boas and sequins   all Max Factor
    size ten stilettos   thigh-high boots
like couture waders   and they're dancing
    they're swirling around   a centripetal bouquet
    they're spidering skeins of light about him
in the chained reflections of their mirror lipgloss

    and the prettiest summons up a hanky
from her pinchbeck cleavage   cups both hands
    surrounds her face and smoothes it clean
    and her skin is perfect ricepaper   beautiful
and barely there   would melt under a tongue
    he thinks   or tear'   and he's afraid

and then she lifts her fingertips
to the starched margin of her bouffant hair
    peels back the flawless label of her face
and inside there's only light   the whitest light
    a weightless light suspending every colour
in its empty net   light you could fall into
and breathe completely   all the way down

    and she reaches her gorgeously manicured hand
to his temple   as if to say *and you?*
but *no no no*   he says   *let's go*
to a drag show   *let's go*   *let's go*

The grey man

The grey man called it auspicious that he die
by night of drowning on a calm sea, the stars
pricking auguries into the black sky.

We buried him on Beacon Hill, the smaller mound
rounding the ridged contour of the larger.
I stayed among the weeds as the sun fell
behind the hilltop, behind the sea, and he –
the grey man – suddenly was there, a shadow
tattered on a rock against the sky.
The signs are auspicious. Your loss may be amended.
Raising my red eyes to the dusk, I asked him how.

The earth shall mother him. At the full moon
unseal a fresh white egg across the mound
and leave the yolk unbroken, for the sun.
Loose a single teardrop, for the sea, and cut
a notch across the lifeline of your palm: let fall
three drops of blood, for the three parts of a tale.
Tell no living soul of what you do,
and do it again, the same, until he rises.

It has been some months, some moons, since then.
Even those who loved him do not go
to Beacon Hill, where seabirds feed on egg.
Alone, I sway there nightly, watching the moon
swing back and forth from hope to desolation.
When it hangs full, I take a new-laid egg,
compress my weeping to a single perfect tear,
unseal once more the lips gashed in my palm.

At home, his eldest swells to fill the gap
his going left; the others seal the edges.
The pain grows in my hand; I cannot weave,
a daughter kneads my bread. I answer
questions and looks askance with silence.
They think me weak, but they bear only grief:
a storm that scours the heart's channels, yet fades
in time to a fisher's breeze along the beach.

What I bear is freight beyond the stoutest beast,
sweet poison, bitter food, a sullen gall of hope
that swells and withers, patterned as the tide,
and draws my blood to follow. I'm lost to hope:
it pins my hands; I cannot hold my grief.
I thin beneath my weather-faded black.
The grey man's not been seen in many weeks.

Waltz

He grips the gather of her waist
and pours her like a ewer into dance.
The blacklist swells of bust and bustle
brim with white-laced imminence –

her body, known by sortilege
alone, its volumes undisclosed,
tonight approximately gauged
through darkness and their civil sleeping-clothes.

Cosmology 101

I *closed*

An indrawn breath, a living volume filled
and emptied, shifting red-shifted stars to blue
(colors of living artery and vein):
a breath, a pulse, a circumnavigation.

II *open*

We plot your arc, project your single span:
to grow, grow colder, thin, and dim, and die;
no covenant, no olive-branch, no ark:
a ghost-ship drifting, no port on your path.

III **undecided**

To hold your breath and guess a course by stars,
each spiral galaxy a silver coin
that's spun to chance, or plan, or fate, and falls
and settles, balanced, magically, on its edge.

The ghost toe

Sebastian was a breech, manhandled forth
by a six-toed foot – his extra toe
(that wanton floret!) the first to test the air.

Six toes? *Who's counting?* His parents knew the score.
The cutters cleft the tiny bone.
A little scar. A perfect little boy.

Last year, Sebastian was told about his toe.
A misguided step! Now Sebastian says
his shoes don't fit. They pinch! They hurt!

At school he feels the ghost toe crammed
in stubborn leather, trodden on in gym.
His slippers tickle! His gumboots rub!

And since his class grew a five-armed starfish
out of a single limb, Sebastian has dreams
where his toe comes back with someone else attached;

and since his captured lizard regrew the tail
it decoyed in the chase, he's quite convinced
his stricken foot is sprouting a replacement:

each night, at bedtime, he checks the scar minutely,
tracing it over and over with a fingertip,
won't sleep without a sock to keep it warm;

and he says, conspiratorially and to everyone,
I got another toe, but you can't see it yet,
it's a special toe. And waits for it to grow.

Three poems

1 *Ice*

I

Cold blue morning. Tiles of ice are laid
with perfect fit to puddles, frost
unhides the webs that chill-curled spiders made.

The tiny spikes on prickleweeds are flossed
with water-crystals, grasses dusted
white with weather; footprints are embossed

along the path where treading broke the crusted
membrane of the night. Afloat
and lambent, fragile particles are mustered

to dance the clouds of breath that clear my throat.
Sunrise slices like a blade
and severed hoarfrost flecks my overcoat.

II

On promising evenings the weatherman said
the night would be freezing, so just before bed,
every winter, once or twice,
we filled a saucer and hoped for ice.

Every winter, once or twice,
We filled a saucer and hoped for ice.

We never had sleet, we never had snow,
and frost was rare and quick to go,
but every winter, once or twice,
we filled a saucer and hoped for ice.

Every winter, once or twice,
We filled a saucer and hoped for ice.

And early next morning we'd check the saucer
And always find it was filled with water,
yet every winter, once or twice,
we filled a saucer and hoped for ice.

Every winter, once or twice,
We filled a saucer and hoped for ice.

III

Through years as blue as sea-ice, striped
with white-thick scars (the cracks that healed
unevenly), observe the scene:

the schoolbag, gymslip, spider-plant
still green (that browned before Grade Two
and died), the Snoopy toy, the puzzle

pieces garbled round the floor,
the half-light seeping through the gap
between the frame and drawn-to door,

the cheeks crushed in his canetoad hand
to mouth a goldfish 'o' (a pout
for him to push his fat prick through):

a picture under glass. And now
a season's silence runs its course.
The sun has risen. Start the thaw.

2 No fairy story

I don't need to tell you what you've done;
I'm sure your memory opens at the thumb
to its favourite page, its pathetic glory:
the centrefold smuggled in a bedtime story.

You played Red King to my Unhappy Princess
and stowed your secrets beneath my mattress:
they kept me awake to the menace of your tread
and mocked the underpants I always wore to bed.

And what can Happy Ever Afters do
when every time I think I've banished you
your thumb slips in and prises me apart,
a staple through my abdomen, another through my heart?

3

I give you words as fierce as fire
I give you voice as heard as ear
    o child –
        my great grief
        my held mute

I give you rooms as new as air
I give you dreams as safe as near
    o child –
        my tight sheaf
        my hard fruit

I give you stop as last as pyre
I give you then as far as fear
    o child –
        my too brief
        my point moot

I give you heart as brave as dare
I give you love as rich as dear
    o child –
        my sole fief
        my deep root

I give you hope as high as spire
I give you home as close as here
    o child –
        my pressed leaf
        my green shoot

Shrew

the tapered nose, an otoscope for a wheatsheaf's ear

lips that don't meet over tiny scimitar teeth

caviar eye-dots, sunk like the knots where buttons were

four clawed feet, screwed into hooks that catch air

fur in tandem streaks of sleek and spiked cat-spit

a splut of puce intestine, looking glued on, no blood

the fine fuse of the tail, that won't be re-lit

Fledging

You were the black bulk over us,
the brooding darkness on the waste:
all beak and talons, bale-red eye,
battening down the sky that lay
beyond the overbearing breast.

Out on a broken limb, we bore
the sullied clutch, the hatch, the fledge,
feathering on the stunted wait
to launch and lyre the singing height
with wing-burled brace, with airful stretch.

I am the cuckoo in the nest,
the wind-up clock, pent on its spring;
my jets are screaming at the brake
and you will feel across your dark
the shadow of my monstrous wing.

Last night at the conference

Midnight. His expertise absently orbits the mole on her left breast.
Large and irregular. Bad news. She should get it checked out.
Nearly the colour and size of her nipple, it squats like a small troll
over her heart. As her doctor he'd order a biopsy – but he
isn't her doctor. He won't look at the rest of her, can't
look at her thighs or the wet curl of her crotch, at her face
strange as the currency furled in his wallet. The snare of the snub mole
captures his eye: it's the one thing he can medicalise.

Only this morning, the mole was a region uncharted in known space.
Somehow, this evening, the universe seems to be spiralling round it,
vortexed by gravity; whole worlds are about to fall in.
Paranoid now, he is whirled by irrational fears that his own wife
felt every slip of his hand, glide of his tongue, felt the harsh
thrust as his blind infidelity broke through the skin of their shared fate,
loosened the seals on the future. He shivers abruptly, then lies still,
tries not to breathe, like a man struck by a snake who attempts
slowing the flow of the poison by slowing the beat of his shocked heart.

Better to be in his own room, where it's quiet and still?
Dressing his body, he's dressing the wounds of this night, but he
      won't seal
arteries pumping his old life to the air with a kiss;
nor will his surgeon's articulate fingers be able to slice out
tumorous falsehood or trim lies from the truth: he's a man
too much aware of himself, or too little.
                  I'm going.
                    The door clicks.
Out in the hallway, he finds that his knees start to shake, puts his
      arm out,
thinks he can see on his skin, faintly, the stain of a mole.

Scales

Now that she's gone they can both see the lies
they told to themselves and each other. Surmise:
what better than love could a species devise
to measure the weight of the scales on its eyes?

The Overall Theory

Nights, while Nana unravelled her knitting,
Poppa found threads that connected things:
apples and xylophones, igloos and id,
paperclips, petioles, Hurricane Joe,
mothballs, dictatorships, us and him.

Poppa could explain most anything:
what paint remover had to do
with buffalo migration, how the moon
had made the bruise on your knee so blue,
why cats were like toothpaste. Poppa knew
Napoleon's link with the Golden Fleece,
how freckles caused earthquakes, and earthquakes caused
what really happened to Aunt Louise.

Poppa was making an Overall Theory
from the bottom up, from a billion things,
he was building a house by filing a cliff
to wear it to sand to make the bricks.
The day he died, our surfer cousin
barrelled through on her way to the beach.
Amanda, my dear, he said, *please tell me
all about wetsuits. I've not factored them in.*

Yode

Do, or do not. There is no try.
    YODA

When the weather's turned bad and you're starting to stall
and there's no way to cancel the launch, recall
the Hindenburg burned and bumblebees fly –
do or do not: there is no try.

When you want it now and you want it all
a windful of pride is much worse than a fall;
you can eat sour grapes or humble pie –
do or do not: there is no try.

When the pressure's as high as the sun is small
a storm in a teacup's a portable squall;
the loveliest courage can lie down and cry –
do or do not: there is no try.

When you're scared of the dark at the end of your hall
but trying to run is forgetting to crawl,
to vanquish your fear is to know how to die –
do or do not: there is no try.

After the funeral

A man's dying is more the survivors' affair than his own.
THOMAS MANN

Here, in a private chapel of the dark,
I curve around your curling back – as though
my flesh could build a denser insulation
over the dance of bones within, and hush
their rattling remembrances; I reach
my planter's hand to reap the love-ploughed contours
moulding your face – as though they could conceal
the human skull's deep anonymity.

Birthday in a new house

The first night passed, my love, we wake today
with boxes all around us, with the sky

a filtered light from unfamiliar angles,
inside a house that's many times our age.

My birthday. Count the crows'-feet of my eyes
that measure time in decades, not in minutes,

that match the pace these filaments of silver
are making in their travel through your hair,

point out to me the fractures in the ceiling,
the hairline cracks that climb the wall, the damp

that flecks the metal window-frames with russet –
tell me the truth, my love. We will not fear

these lines that spread the messages of age
through lath and plaster, hair and skin; we know

that no house stands forever, but that love
can hold a house together long enough.

Three dreams about the river

I *The horse*

Wanting home, you find
the swollen river is gumming the bridge.
Along the bank, there's a sodden path
and square across the path is a horse,
impassive, massive, fetlocks in the water.
You somehow know those draggled shins
want to knock you in.

II *The boat*

You're sat aboard
a long tourist boat, that you don't know
has no motor, floating with the river.
This isn't so bad, you say,
now you're underway.

III *The river*

No path, no boat,
just the river and you in it,
in it and of it, a sleek thing
whose pelt opens a path like a seal's.
Translucent, nearly as clear as the water,
you loop a cursive joy through the current,
inscribe the avowal of being alive,
when you arrive

at the open mouth
where the whole sweet flow goes underground
for a distance, forever, who knows? – but there
not even the river itself could tell
which dappled silver ripple was you
as you pass through.

Melbourne, evening, summertime –

the flies settling, passing the torch
of insect purpose to moths, mosquitoes
(the night-shift's proletariat); the sun
now tucking in until the morning, furling
the eucalpyt linen of clean blue ranges
to its chin; the murmured benedicite
of late sea breezes to the exorcised heat;

and we, alone on lawns, or jointly laid
in the mitred corners of urban parks,
curled in deckchairs, swingchairs, armchairs,
rocked on bayside boats, or dieselling home
on end-of-workday tractors as the mendicant sky
sums up its last small change of sun,

we find our warmth in evening's cool,
see drawn like sweat our gentlest selves,
are loosed to float on the slow emotions
stirred by twilight and the rightness of things.

A prayer

She holds me naked in her natal hand,
unfurling me like wheat-seed in the rain:
o hold your fingers close, for I am sand.

And when my stricken ear must understand
the dirge beneath the drumming of the vein,
she holds me fragile in her faithful hand:

o confiscate the heart's hard contraband,
the worm, the creeping fracture in the pane –
o hold your fingers close, for I am sand.

And as the dark foreshadows its demand
and dogs the dwindling bounds of my domain,
she holds me weary in her watchful hand:

o let me bind the days already spanned
like garlands round the hours that remain –
o hold your fingers close, for I am sand.

And as the harvest gathers on the land,
and as the sickle scythes across the grain,
she holds me silent in her simple hand:
o let your fingers fall, for I am sand.

On our hands
(for Patrick)

This evening, as you touch my arm, again
I see the strange alikeness of our hands:
your hand is my hand, swelled into a man's;
two sketches, on two scales, of one terrain.
And now you take a pencil, tilt the light,
and borrowing my writing paper, lined
in feint-rule blue, you move that hand to find
the contours of my face across the white.
If I could only touch your hand and take
your gentle skill in my like hand, I'd draw
my mirror vision of the portraiture
that only love and skill conjoined can make –
but even in this clumsy hand of mine
your face is framed in love across these lines.

On your shoulders

On bramble-stalks that arc above my head
in thunderclouds the ripened blackberries hang,
the harder fruit in clustered beads of blood,
red hints of thorns that ward the bush's young.
You bend and fit your shoulders to my thighs
and bear me up; my twice-extended arm
outdares the thorns to break the bush's prise:
your lips take blood and berries from my palm.
This evening, in the twined sheets of our bed
below the arching eaves, I'll elevate
your body by the depth of mine instead,
be nourished as you trust me with your weight
as gently as a womb's red lining swells
to cup a little blackberry of cells.

Ultrasound at 13 weeks

A child, I'd curl up small at night
in moonlight's brittle calm
and make believe I rested safe
within a giant palm.

This bell of muscle rings you round
as never fingers could
until the birthday when you come
to claim your personhood;

for now, this image speaks for you:
a snowflake hand outflung
proclaiming *human*, greeting us
in every human tongue.

Breath

Is it pure cinema now, the mirror
held to the lips of a dying man –
that truth-revealing glass in which
the ceding life can't see itself,
only the mist ghost of the breath?

These winter nights, the wet of our breath
mists on the window-pane in cauls
scored by the breadth of falling beads.
We wake to the unmistakable trace
of life: this glass we can't see through.

He says no

The night before the first course
he strafed his own head to a spare fuzz,
burned the fallen strands in a flat dish
with oak leaves and rosemary.
The stubble came away inside a week,
spiking his pillow and palms, ungatherable.

The first course failed, a big slug
to the odds, but they pressed him on.
He took it again, flat on his back
for the fat cannula, desperate measures
drip-fed to his chastened veins.
The second treatment also failed.

Ready to stop, he was beaten down
by the brandished advice of specialists,
pinned on the tines of his anxious family:
but here on the ward, prepped and bedded
for another dose of toxic Maybe,
he comes to himself. Says *No. No more.*

He ports his sick frame to the highlands
where spring comes late, but comes anyway,
spatters grace on the hills' shaved curves.
For a while the phone hums with rumours
of miracle cures, but he demurs
politely, not at all unsure:

he's found his transient medicines –
his strewn hills, his veers of earth
all bare and limblike, limber and awake,
his yet-green oak-trunk cored to a husk
by fungus, full of light; all these
are a bootstrap redemption. An answer. His own.

You visit, ask how he is. He smiles,
fingers the twin scarred ridges on his nails
that gloss like tree rings, telling history,
holds out the baffled stigma of his happiness
and says to you *I know who I am*,
and you see it in his face. He does. Yes.

·

The night before the last day of January

will be remembered by a random few
for having borne it out in sheeted snow
on no exceptional stretch of motorway,
rationing the engine's gas-and-air
to intervals of heat while still more snow
slipped down, unprecedented, otherworldly;

but I'll recall it as the unslept night
before that morning-after when you lay
against my heart on the white of ward-square sheets:
a little snowflake fallen into warmth,
fragile, precise, astoundingly unmelting.

(for Caitlin, b. 31.01.03)

The raptor in winter

above the snow
a shingled limb
fractures the sky
of frozen blue

taut as a bud
a raptor waits
upon its length
unmoved until

led by his sense
he launches from
this lichened perch
to hang in air

folds in his wings
and simply falls
his being become
pure cynosure

and in his drop
this utter will
extends beyond
his taloned reach

senses the earth
and pulls him back
from plummet's end
as ever before

still mastering
the ageless pull
of earth for life
he yet will serve

Tails

The silvered windows at Tullamarine
glowed with a travelling red-gold flush,
the mirrored skim of the sun's dawn disk
that fired the skin of the incoming planes.

My own plane, out there, closing in,
was winding up our wait like a reel.
The minutes hung on a shortening line
I could not lengthen; nor could I unwind

your shrinking, tightening curl of spine
that suddenly craned to the floor, pulled back
a tiny payload, Queen's head tailed
by a coiled echidna: five Australian cents.

Here you are, dear: that little gain
a talisman to loss, you passed it on,
and silence spoke beneath our voices then,
the bones of your hand enclosed in mine.

Through the passengers' gate, gripping your coin
like a cool change to the flame of my palm,
Tails, I thought, *and I'll see you again*,
but didn't toss, no, couldn't toss that coin.

I learned something recently. Did you know
echidnas dig themselves to ground in fire?
The firefront passes, and through smoking earth
a spine foretells the phoenix ashy beast.

I saw this in a film and thought of you,
your windfall coin, your own grey ash
in a funeral garden braced by gums,
those hungry, grey-green, fire-feeding trees.

The coin I've kept – you'd laugh, I know –
on the inside lid of my writing tin,
silvering the pens' red, black, green, grey,
and on those sweet rare days when the words
come deeper than voice, I flip the lid
to take my pen, and there it is: Tails.

Home

Beside me on the couch, the cat, asleep,
types a soliloquy in twitching feet.
Your shoulder's warm, our baby breathes above;
some wounds need no remedy but love.